Vampire HAIKU

Ryan Mecum

HOW BOOKS

Cincinnati, Ohio

www.howdesign.com

For more excellent books and resources for designers, visit www.howdesign.com.

13 12 11 10 09   5 4 3 2 1

Distributed in Canada by Fraser Direct, 100 Armstrong Avenue, Georgetown, Ontario, Canada L7G 5S4, Tel: (905) 877-4411. Distributed in the U.K. and Europe by David & Charles, Brunel House, Newton Abbot, Devon, TQ12 4PU, England, Tel: (+44) 1626-323200, Fax: (+44) 1626-323319, E-mail: postmaster@ davidandcharles.co.uk. Distributed in Australia by Capricorn Link, P.O. Box 704, Windsor, NSW 2756 Australia, Tel: (02) 4577-3555

Library of Congress Cataloging-in-Publication Data

Mecum, Ryan.
 Vampire haiku / Ryan Mecum.
   p. cm.
  ISBN 978-1-60061-772-0 (pbk : alk. paper)
  1. Haiku—Humor. 2. Vampires—Humor. I. Title.
  PN6231.H28 M427 2009
  818'.607—dc22

                              2009008167

Editor: Amy Schell
HOW Books Art Director: Grace Ring
Production Coordinator: Greg Nock

Designer/Packager:
Lisa Kuhn/Curio Press, LLC
www.curiopress.com

This journal belongs to

William Butten

W. Butten

September 16th, 1620

Red sunlight burns through
with the approaching new dawn.
Time for me to go.

Today we embark
from our world to a new land
on the Mayflower.

Dear haiku journal,
My name is William Butten,
age one-and-twenty.

Five syllables first,
then followed by seven more,
and then five again.

I will document
all my New World adventures
into small poems.

While loading the boat,
I notice some packed coffins.
Pessimistic bunch.

As the ship leaves land
in the cool September mist,
seagulls sing farewell.

What adventures lie
  on this ocean's other side?
Life to the fullest!

The fog envelops.
As our country disappears,
  the seagulls turn back.

September 22nd, 1620

On the deck at night
as thousands of stars shine down,
I see her, alone.

A married woman,
        undeniably stunning;
likes to flirt with me.

Like a siren song,
each night she calls me to her
    and I am in love.

In the glassy sea,
she, I, and the moon reflect.
Hers is a bit ... off.

Our first kiss was bad,
for when she began necking,
      I began bleeding.

    Katherine Carver,
     gorgeous wife of John Carver,
drank blood from my neck.

    I did not realize
     I was dying at the time,
but I died that night.

Much to my surprise,
as she pulled back from my neck,
I bit into hers.

With main arteries,
you have to be well prepared
for the instant gush.

Keep your mouth on tight,
lips firmly pressed against skin.
(Due to the spurting.)

I should be careful.
Accidental tongue biting
just got easier.

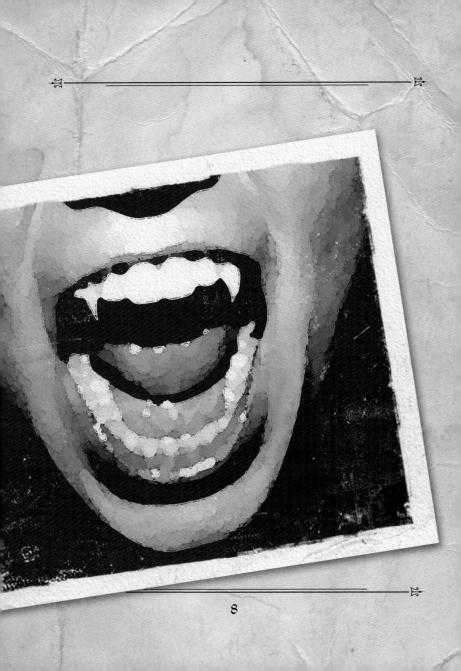

Katherine explains,
as I stare at her red fangs,
what I have become.

We kill to survive,
drink the warm blood of humans,
and tanning is bad.

She uses new words,
like calling our kind "vampires,"
not "crazed murderers."

The syllable count
for "vampire" is confusing.
Two? Three? I'll guess two.

The thought of killing
normally would appall me.
Now it sounds pleasant.

Follow a few rules
and I can live forever.
Seems like a good trade.

Katherine is old.
My great-great-great grandmother
would be near her age.

She explains to me
that wood through my heart will kill.
I don't think that's new.

We can become bats.
    I think she is just joking;
then she starts flapping.

        Her bat: less "rodent,"
    more "giant black-winged demon."
    "Bat" seems like a stretch.

        This girl with bat wings
flies us above the ocean
    and I grow wings, too.

        Wings rip through clothing:
        If I try this trick again,
        I should cut shirt slits.

With day approaching
     we go to the cargo hold,
because now, day kills.

Seeing my new bed
stirs a fear I'll have to kick—
claustrophobia.

To ensure no sun,
most vampires sleep in coffins.
A bit dramatic.

September 23rd, 1620

Vampire John Carver
   wakes me from my coffin—
to teach me some tricks.

How to eat someone:
Hold tight, bite neck, suck hard, drink.
   Repeat as needed.

Ed Thompson becomes
   the first Mayflower deceased,
and John Carver's lunch.

You might be surprised
how little it takes to kill
when you are thirsty.

I start off easy.
A small boy named Jasper More
I drink like water.

Blood tastes like cherries
mixed with a lot of copper
and way too much salt

March 28th, 1621

Once we got to land,
just four were killed on the boat.
Five if you count me.

John wants the vampires
to populate this country.
I just want his wife.

When there's three vampires
with odd social dynamics,
two might be better.

If you are in love
with a married vampire girl,
make her a widow.

April 4th, 1621

John and I go out
hunting under the new moon
with different goals.

He eats his last meal,
although he doesn't know it—
then I knock him out.

Tied between two pines
with open sky above him,
I leave him for dawn.

Our confused doctor
    declares another odd death.
John died by sunstroke.

Getting a sunburn
has a whole new meaning now.
    A lot less desired.

April 7th, 1621

His crispy body,
back in his sleeping coffin,
was buried at night.

I don't get women.
I go and murder for love
and she's mad at me.

We get in a fight
which ends with her kissing me.
I did the right thing.

She says she loves me,
but killing John was stupid,
and now they'll find us.

The vampire hunters,
which apparently exist,
will know she is here.

Using an old corpse,
Katherine fakes her demise
and then disappears.

I would look for her
but she'll miss me soon enough—
and pilgrims taste good.

I'm in no hurry.
    Not getting any younger
nor any older.

November 22nd, 1622

It's a harsh winter.
Many die due to illness—
or that's what they think.

Although half are dead,
they share food in thanksgiving.
I already ate.

They give thanks to God
for their squash, corn and livestock.
I give thanks for them.

May 23rd, 1688

Flying is easy—
if, when you want to try it,
wings grow from your back.

I don't bathe as much
because flying fast through clouds
gets me pretty clean.

When a mosquito
pierces my neck and drinks blood,
is that irony?

I play with my food
by sucking blood through the holes,
then blowing it back.

Why does garlic hurt?
If your senses were heightened,
it would hurt you, too.

June 3rd 1693

The Salem Witch Hunt.
The Salem Vampire Hunt.
It's all semantics.

All I know is this—
I tried to kill some people
and some girls got blamed.

Were the girls witches
or possessed by the devil?
Tasted fine to me.

March 18th, 1717

My favorite perk
        of eternally cold skin—
    bye-bye sweaty pits!

        Vampire friends of mine
    sometimes hang out at my place
        and stay up all day.

            The neck artery
    is the most normal to bite.
        Between toes is weird.

            My conscience is clear.
            It's not me that kills people,
        it's the loss of blood.

September 9th, 1752

Drinking by myself
from a lonely bartender,
missing Katherine.

She never came back,
   but by the way she bit me—
I know it's true love.

               Like hide-and-go-seek,
all America inbounds,
               she is hard to find.

I'm always looking,
      hoping to run into her—
take her out for necks.

November 19th, 1774

A revolution
that leads to war and bloodshed
is like one long meal.

Many massacres
other than the Boston one
took place in the streets.

The Boston harbor
had more than just dumped taxed tea
in the bay that night.

A sigh of relief.
     The Intolerable Acts
are not about me.

More people like me
arrive with hopes of a war,
     helping to provoke.

Redcoats line the road.
Patriots hide in the woods,
and vampires above.

After the battle,
we fly down and pick at scraps
like thirsty vultures.

My coat looks like theirs.
While eating in my tan one,
it quickly turns red.

I hardly need fangs.
Bayonet wounds to the neck
make easy access.

You should drink slowly
and filter between your teeth,
in case of bullets.

We all feast for hours
but leave before the sunrise,
and food goes to waste.

August 4th, 1799

Retractable fangs
take greater concentration
than wiggling my ears.

The tip of my tooth
is a constant distraction
for my restless tongue.

There must be a way
to pierce through somebody's neck
without staining shirts.

Newer wounds don't scar,
so this scar from childhood
means a lot to me.

Yet another perk
of turning at a young age:
I'll never go bald.

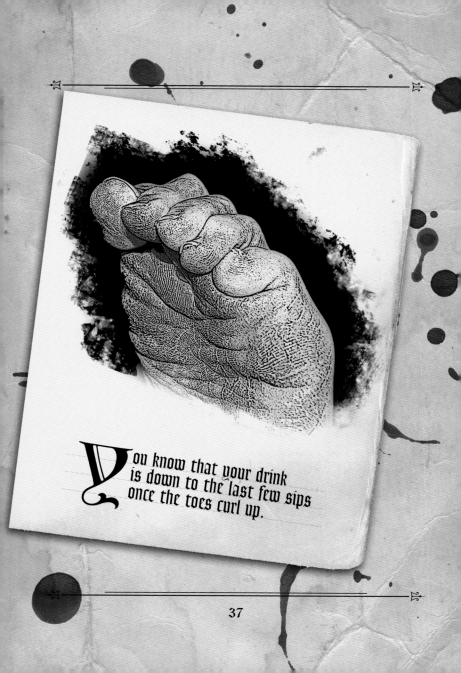

You know that your drink
is down to the last few sips
once the toes curl up.

July 5th, 1807

Washington, DC:
As fireworks lit up the streets,

I saw Katherine.

She was in the crowd,
hunting for what I was, too—
sweet crimson nectar.

She saw me and grinned,
as I crossed the busy street,
then reached to hug me.

With an awkward joke,
"Keep your mouth off of my neck!"
I pulled her to me.

After we caught up,
we went out to have some fun.
By "fun," I mean "blond."

As the night died down,
I asked Katherine simply
to never leave me.

"I'm sorry," she said.
"It's called Independence Day.
Maybe try next year."

July 5th, 1808

Well, I tried this year.
Couldn't find her in the crowd.
Maybe next year then.

July 5th, 1809

Every year I'll try
searching through the crowd for her.
Something to live for.

I know she was here.
The paper had a story
about some odd deaths.

March 25th, 1836

Whenever they say
"Remember the Alamo,"
my mouth salivates.

Some people wonder,
How did Davy Crockett die?
The answer: Screaming.

Although Davy died,
he drank blood from my neck too,
so he's still around.

We got along well,
so next time I'm in Texas
I'll look Davy up.

July 5th, 1845

Washington again.
No Katherine anywhere.
No reason to live.

It was hard to see.
I kicked over some fireworks
which lit up the crowd.

October 23rd, 1855

If there's too much air,
it turns from a soup to paste.
Blood can quickly clot.

This is something worse
than continuous hunger—
continuous thirst.

I only need blood,
but sometimes I eat apples.
Well ... Adam's apples.

A fun winter drink—
hot blood mixed with a cold neck—
I've nicknamed Frost Bite.

All things considered,
I'm glad we turn into bats.
Leeches drink blood, too.

Blood can geyser out,
if you twist the necks just right,
like water fountains.

No threat of sunlight
breaking through the coffin box.
My favorite place.

Though clearly creepy—
despite evil foreboding—
coffins are comfy.

September 27th, 1862

My country at war:
When 600,000 die,
eating gets easy.

I fought for the South,
and when they started losing,
I switched to the North.

Lots of blood to drink
the night after long battles;
fields full of bodies.

The rivers ran red,
which led to moonlit swimming
with my mouth open.

Battlefield dinners.
The Antietam leftovers
kept me full for weeks.

July 18th, 1862

I messed with a girl,
        a poet named Emily,
    who called me Master.

I couldn't touch her
until she made one mistake—
    inviting me in.

She was protected,
    surrounded by a bubble
    of her garlic breath.

The small cross necklace
that dangles in between us
    makes slow dancing odd.

Pregnant woman blood
is a drink I steer clear from.
Makes my hormones weird.

When pregnant girls turn,
their fetuses also turn,
but never come out.

The pregnant vampires—
with eternal parasites—
are always moody.

She would always say
that she couldn't stop for death,
so I stopped for her.

First I broke her heart,
followed by self confidence.
Then I let her live.

Her morbid poems
grew darker as we dated.
I messed her up good.

A narrow fellow
who will unbraid in the sun—
pretty sure that's me.

After I broke her,
she turned her back on the world.
Rarely left the house.

July 13th, 1865

A circus showman,
　　　Phineas Taylor Barnum,
offered me a job.

He was a smart man
who had somehow figured out
what I really am.

His staff was unique—
　　a collection of people
not quite like people.

He would pay me well
    if I would sit in a tent
and just flap my wings.

When I turned him down,
    he said he wasn't upset:
He'd find another.

"There's a sucker born,"
    he told me, about vampires,
"every minute."

I let Barnum live
    but burned down his museum.
He got the message.

October 8th, 1871

I found Katherine
    on a farm in Illinois
with a new last name.

As she ran away,
    she threw a lantern at me,
    but it hit a cow.

The barn caught on fire,
    (as did most of Chicago),
and she got away.

December 30th, 1890

Fighting over land.
Cowboys killing Indians
leads to fields of blood.

We have a saying:
Never cry over spilt blood.
Just get down and lick.

Blood mixing in dirt
becomes chewing tobacco
I keep in my lip.

Custer's real last stand,
post-Little Bighorn feasting,
was in my bowels.

Later on that night,
the battle at Wounded Knee
led to wounded necks.

May 26th, 1897

Bad news for my kind:
A new "tell-all" hit the shelves.
Bram Stoker must die!

Smart vampire fiction
is usually created
by those who hunt us.

Some vampires believe
Stoker tells Van Helsing fans
how to destroy us.

If I find Stoker,
I'd bottle his blood like wine
for special events.

November 14th, 1924

Yum, tasty hors d'oeuvres!
Fast-running barefoot victims
get big blood blisters.

Most vampires are pale,
but complementing colors
work undead wonders.

Since I don't see it,
a bright sun seems like a myth;
like I am to some.

Permanent bedhead—
one of the difficulties
of not reflecting.

Excluding brooding,
the vampire stereotype:
Mostly on the mark.

We can't all seduce.
Big, fat and hairy vampires—
not too seductive.

Sometimes, to relax,
I'll bring a girl to my place
and take a bloodbath.

We're not full of lust,
contrary to our image.
Well, bloodlust, maybe.

Only one meaning
of "Go for the jugular"
applies when hunting.

I have always thought
blood is thicker than water
and more refreshing.

*An odd truth I've learned:
People up past 3 a.m.
are always no good.*

The Great Depression.
Great for making more homeless;
not too depressing.

During troubled times
when the world seems shaken up,
we vampires eat well.

Flimsy little homes,
which some folks call Hoovervilles,
I call lunchboxes.

Prohibition laws
against addictive drinking
are not new to me.

I love the homeless.
They don't have to invite me
to enter alleys.

People without homes—
like they are expecting me—
don't put up much fight.

So many homeless.
Police can't protect them all.
I can be messy.

October 1st, 1932

I love the Yankees.
A baseball player named George
is my favorite.

One night I told him,
if he wins the World Series,
his family lives.

I went to Game 3,
hid in the center field shade,
and watched through blankets.

When he was at bat,
he pointed his hand at me,
and hit me the ball.

It was a great game.
I let his family live
and left him alone.

June 10th, 1937

It wasn't the crash.
Amelia Earhart was killed
        because of sunlight.

Flying in a plane
with the sun chasing behind,
        she didn't make it.

Attempt two killed her.
    She already circled once,
but in her bat form.

As a skilled vampire,
she was known for her flying
long before airplanes.

During the crusades,
they all called her "Amelia,
Baby Impaler."

The world mourned her death.
If they knew the true Earhart,
there would be fireworks.

Search parties went out,
but they would never find her
unless they searched Hell.

December 7th, 1946

Flying over zoos,
vulnerable giraffe necks
are hard to pass up.

I brush twice a day.
My teeth are real important.
Tooth decay can kill.

A Bloody Mary,
or a Bloody Anyone,
is my choice cocktail.

Blood in my urine
doesn't mean I'm really sick.
It just means I'm full.

My tongue has trouble
licking the blood off my lips
due to my sharp teeth.

Mostly, pools of blood
are actually just puddles.
A pool would be great!

September 30th, 1955

I fly above cars
that race through California
in the desert night.

If the car top's down,
a rebel without a cause
makes for good eating.

I pluck his body
up into the desert sky,
which makes his car crash.

After I drink him,
I drop his body back down
into the car flames.

I should be careful:
Last night's car crash meal made news.
Guess he was famous.

The newspaper says
a death wish was in his blood.
I didn't taste it.

June 20th, 1965

I met an author
who I thought would be my friend.
Another phony.

J.D. Salinger
lost interest in many things
after I bit him.

Now he sits alone;
never leaves his apartment.
Gets blood delivered.

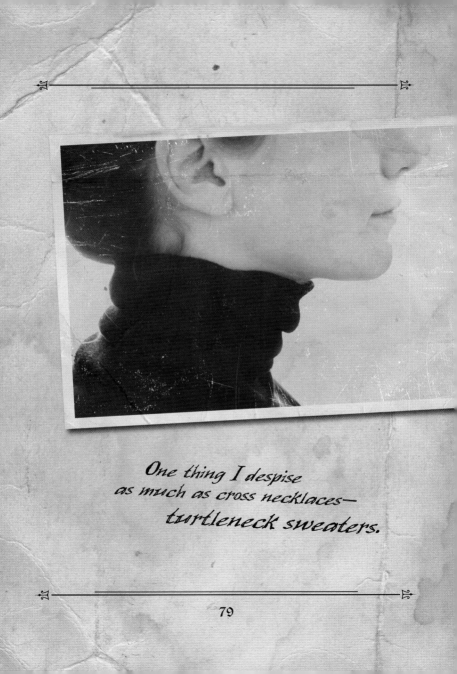

One thing I despise
as much as cross necklaces—
turtleneck sweaters.

April 3rd, 1967

Garlic breath, to me
is more deadly than stinky;
more like napalm breath.

The Vietnam War—
not bizarre unsolved murders—
fills the newspapers.

I dodge peace protests.
Hundreds march with wooden stakes.
Peace signs can kill me.

There are pros and cons
when I attack church blood drives.
Pro: blood drive. Con: church.

Church water fountains:
Maybe that's holy water?
I don't go near them.

Some people complain
if Communion wine is juice.
I complain at wine.

Some crucifixes
can hurt me more than others.
It's all about size.

A cross is a cross
if that is its intention.
Crossing beams don't count.

A cross only works
if the person holding it
believes it will work.

A stake through the lung,
although it doesn't kill me,
really hurts like hell.

You would be surprised—
the amount of wooden stakes
that are in most rooms.

Upside-down death spikes,
like sitting on loaded guns:
a chair with wood legs.

August 16th, 1969

    I'm at a concert
somewhere in northern New York.
Clothing optional.

All the posters said
"3 days of peace & music."
Well, they got half right

    Lots of these people
say they'll try anything once.
This is too easy.

Woodstock fields at night.
Peace, love and passed out bodies:
a vampire buffet.

I'm seeing double.
These people are so drugged up.
Their blood makes me *weird*.

These people are so drugged up.
Their blood makes me *weird*.

I'm seeing double.
These people are so drugged up.
Their blood makes me *weird*.

January 19, 1972

Like a piece of gum,
I can chew on them for hours—
rubbery blood clots.

Different blood types
each have a unique flavor.
I'm a fan of O.

Almost every time,
a B positive blood type
leads to a bad pun.

Sometimes I hang out
outside emergency rooms;
get some blood work done.

The homeless people
in New York subway tunnels:
emergency snacks.

The vampires I know
who actually wear black capes
are not that scary.

I don't have to breathe,
but I like holes in coffins
for ventilation.

May 31st, 1975

For my vacations,
    I always pick Kentucky
for its mining caves.

            Sometimes I would cause
                coal mining caves to collapse;
                    me inside with them.

With everyone stuck,
    and no sunrise time limit,
I can feast in peace.

            The more you scare them
            the more they run all around,
                using up their air.

To time it just right,
    drink your last dying miner
as help shovels through.

July 5th, 1976

The fireworks rattle
the Washington Monument
as I perch on top.

The National Mall,
once again filled with people,
many drinks-to-be.

Somehow I see her.
Alone in the massive crowd:
Katherine my love.

She can't believe it.
Says the sun should have got me,
as we laugh and spin.

We walk arm in arm
along the Reflecting Pool
without reflecting.

A drunk man joins us
inside a porta-pottie,
but does not come out.

I am so in love.
I can feel my long-dead heart
trying to warm up.

"Not this year, either,"
she says as she backs away
and blows me a Kiss.

December 28th, 1977

Some want to be bit.
A guy in New York City
begged me to turn him.

I told him I would—
If he brought me blood all year,
I'd make him my son.

So he worked for me.
I didn't tell him my name
but he called me Sam.

It worked for a while.
Now he's in prison for life.
Fun while it lasted.

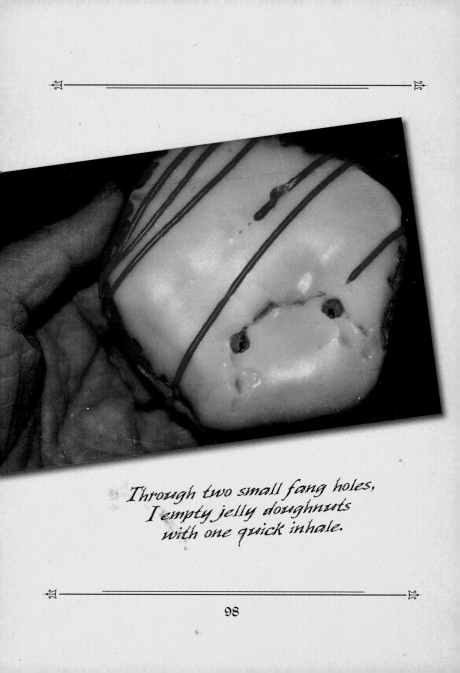

Through two small fang holes,
I empty jelly doughnuts
with one quick inhale.

April 29th, 1985

It's taken some time.
Now I can finish a drink
with my chin still clean.

Prank phone calls are fun.
I ask for blood donations,
then go pick them up.

Hanging upside down:
How would that be relaxing?
Sounds like a headache.

Silver burns my skin
like some vampire eczema.
I've got lube for it.

Like a juice box straw,
it's hard to suck through knee veins.
Aim for arteries.

"You are my sunshine ..."
(the scariest song ever)
"... my only sunshine."

What's with the hissing
found in vampire pop culture?
Perhaps bad fake fangs.

Now I've seen it all.
Vampire puppets on TV
teaching kids to count.

On each Halloween
I dress as Count Dracula.
I've heard he does, too.

March 1st, 1993

I found an old friend
Davy from the Alamo.
Now he's called David.

It had been decades,
 so he invited me down
to his place to drink.

Still lived in Texas;
 some Branch Davidian ranch
just outside Waco.

He lived like a King!
He tricked all these families
to live there with him.

Each night he would choose—
and families would let him—
a different neck.

He felt safe in forts.
This one was Alamo-like,
except filled with girls.

It didn't last long,
thanks to politics and cops,
but we lived it up.

Like a déjà vu,
as the guns surrounded us,
Davy and I smiled.

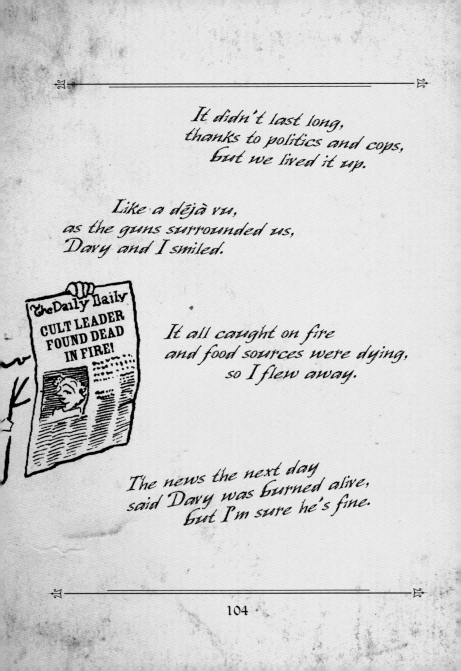

It all caught on fire
and food sources were dying,
so I flew away.

The news the next day
said Davy was burned alive,
but I'm sure he's fine.

April 2nd, 1998

My favorite show
stars the cutest little girl
who slays fake vampires.

This show creator
understands the vampire world
abnormally well.

I have heard legend
of an actual slayer
who hunts real vampires.

If a little girl
tried to kill me with a stake,
I'd eat her like steak.

Kids with their lingo.
When they say that something sucks,
I just get hungry.

Some normal humans
will act like they are vampires,
like kids who play house.

The fake vampire boys
listen to "hard-core" rock bands,
but wear mascara.

Most all real vampires
prefer classical music—
and maybe Tom Waits.

All the gothic kids,
in black jeans, jackets and boots,
cry when I bite them.

July 24th, 1999

Another Woodstock,
trading love for flames and fights,
but the same great taste.

Money's no problem.
Dead people don't need wallets,
so I'm doing well.

Across the country,
     I own many apartments
     with windows blacked out.

The best apartments
are both soundproof and sunproof,
     with drains in the floors.

Though I don't eat it,
     I often display a box
     of Count Chocula.

Blood bags in the fridge
     and a coffin on the floor
make my home sweet home.

May 28th, 2004

Whoa! This one went quick!
If they're taking blood thinners,
one suck and all gone.

Always startling—
dark rooms instantly blinding
with fluorescent lights.

I've been sleeping less
due to the hi-def flat screen
inside my coffin.

Despite what you'd think,
tanning beds do not kill me—
but so expensive!

Discarded band-aids
are rare unexpected treats.
My version of gum.

If I drink too much,
    oxygen is like caffeine:
I'll be up all day.

Music	hemophiliacs
Movies	Nick Cave, James Marsters
Television	Anything with Bill Paxton
Books	Not Blade
Heroes	Bunnicula
	Vlad Tepes

During the daytime,
behind cardboarded windows,
there's not much to do.

Checking the menu,
officially called MySpace,
for a bite to eat.

Sitting on my couch, flipping through all the channels, drinking a bloodbag.

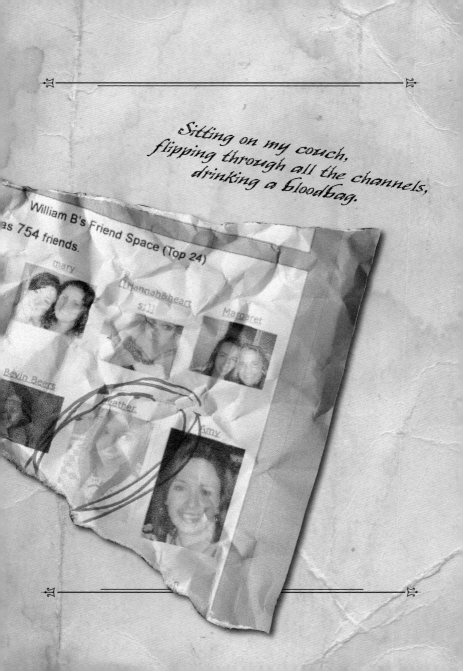

William B's Friend Space (Top 24)

...as 754 friends.

mary

[[Hannah&heart

sill

Margaret

Bevin Beers

Heather

Amy

December 4th, 2008

Today brings sad news:
Forrest J. Ackerman died.
Vampirella cries.

I have never met
(though a fun pop culture trend)
a noble vampire.

Most vampire movies—
which are often called "horror"—
I call "comedy."

I just saw Twilight
It's labeled a vampire film,
but I don't know why.

Those were not vampires.
If sunlight makes you sparkle,
you're a unicorn.

The underage girl
and century-old dead guy,
awkwardly in love.

If this were real life,
Ed would have looked at her neck—
bite, dead, burp, credits.

Batman & Robin
was not Joel Shumacher's worst:
He made The Lost Boys.

Rarely has a film
made me want to jump in it
and kill the whole cast.

If the Frog brothers
tried to stake me through the heart—
frog legs for dinner.

What would be better
than biting on a Corey?
Biting two Coreys.

One film that's alright,
though I don't get the title,
sounds like "gesundheit"

The name of the film
should be said after sneezes.
"Hachoo!" "Nosferatu."

The only movie
that portrays the vampire well:
Bigelow's Near Dark.

"Let's put it this way.
I fought for the South. We lost."
Lance Henriksen rules!

Tom Cruise and Brad Pitt.
This is horror movie stuff?
Bela Lugosi!

July 5th, 2009

Again in DC,
looking for the one I love
and one to get bit

I love only her—
only her and drinking blood—
not sure the order.

Centuries later,
I have only reminisced.
One lone memory.

When Katherine bit,
everything around me died
and there was just us.

I have felt no joy
since the night she murdered me—
nor have I missed it.

True intimacy
     is allowing a lover
to rip out your heart.

Looking everywhere,
     I just want her to see me
and know I'm still here.

Someone taps my back,
and I twirl around to find
Katherine crying.

Though we're in a crowd,
all the walking bags of blood
vanish when we hug.

Apologizing,
she says our hunter is near.
She's being followed.

I pull her with me
inside a nearby building
for some privacy.

The people guarding
the Washington Monument
don't see us fly past.

The tower is closed
and we talk in the darkness
as we climb the steps.

A hunter of us—
a true vampire murderer—
is here in the crowd.

She tells me sorry;
that she's tried to protect me
and that she loves me.

"We could never be.
We draw too much attention
whenever we play."

"One of us would die
and the pain would be too great
for the one that's left."

We hear sharp footsteps,
and we both know who's coming—
Death climbs up the stairs.

Teeth sharp, hands ready,
we both dive down to greet him
as fireworks explode.

He mumbles, "Grr, Arg,"
and Joss the Vampire Slayer
greets us with a smile.

"Funny place to fight,"
he says as we attack him.
"The world's largest stake."

He and Katherine,
an entangled raging ball,
roll down the staircase.

They are both screaming.
She wants me to fly away.
He wants me to watch.

Her greatest weapon
has always been her beauty,
not her combat skills.

Racing after them,
fangs out and feet off the steps,
I know it's too late.

With one sharp motion,
I watch him thrust down a stake
into Katherine.

She slips down a step,
turns from vampire into girl,
and then smiles at me.

With a fleeting glance,
what was once my beloved
crumbles into ash.

Everything I love
softly floats up through the air.
Her dust covers me.

He turns to face me,
but revenge is meaningless
when everything's dead.

I fly down the steps
and he just watches me go
out into the night.

Wanting Katherine
is what has kept me alive—
not just all the blood.

Katherine is gone.
America is nothing.
I should go now, too.

The crowd disperses
and the fireworks are over.
There is nothing left.

Like a stone gargoyle,
I sit on the White House roof
and write all this down.

I dangle my feet
above the East side entrance
and watch the sky turn.

It's been a long time,
since the last time I sat down
to watch the sunrise.

If my heart could beat
it would have skipped one or two
as red pierces though.

Crimson rays above
and the clouds glow like a fire.
Smells like I am, too.

As I'm writing this,
my syllable-counting hand
is starting to smoke.

And then it hits me—
vampires are so dramatic—
this will really hurt.

Letting myself bake
is not why Katherine died.
I am not finished.

If I can get up
and preserve her in my heart,
our love will go on.

She created me
and her creation will live
with her memory.

This country shivers
and I want to suck its blood.
I am born anew!

Old ragged journal,
this part of my life is through.
And I'm through with you.

I'm leaving you here
and I'm off to find some shade.
You are on your own.

Dear haiku journal,
remember William Butten,
three centuries old.

Red sunlight burns through
with the approaching new dawn.
Time for me to go.

About the Design

Vampire Haiku is designed by Lisa Kuhn, owner of Curio Press, located in Cincinnati, Ohio. Curio Press is devoted to high quality book design and packaging.

For more information visit:
www.curiopress.com

curio press llc

About the Author

Ryan Mecum likes to write poems about monsters. Vampire Haiku is the second book of Ryan's Horror Haiku series. He also wrote Zombie Haiku. He has a degree in English from the University of Cincinnati, has twice run a mile in four minutes and twenty-nine seconds, and has been flipped off by Kurt Cobain. Ryan lives in Cincinnati, Ohio, with his wife and daughter.

For more information about Ryan Mecum, please visit: www.ryanmecum.com.

Dedicated to Tony:
All those Tuesday nights racing home to watch Buffy, long before Tivo.

ALSO CHECK OUT
ZOMBIE HAIKU
BY RYAN MECUM

Biting into heads
is much harder than it looks.
the stuff is feisty.

Within hurts one man.
Normal the screwdriver
wouldn't have gone here.

You are so lucky
that I cannot remember
how to use doorknobs.

ISBN: 978-1-60061-070-7,
144 PAGES, PAPERBACK, $9.99, #Z1805

"The most inventive zombie book in years!"
DAVID WELLINGTON, MONSTER ISLAND

"A thoroughly unique and entertaining experience. Ryan Mecum has quite possibly found the only corner of entertainment not yet infected by the zombie plague—haiku—and made me wonder why it took this long, as the two seem to go together like zombies and brains. I highly recommend it to fans of all things zombie."
ROBERT KIRKMAN, THE WALKING DEAD AND MARVEL ZOMBIES

"Ryan Mecum obviously knows his zombie films well, and his book tells a gory, violent story that will warm the veins of Romero fans."
RUE MORGUE MAGAZINE

"...the art of Haiku has been cannibalized by Ryan Mecum in his original graphic novel ZOMBIE HAIKU and the result is simply one of the best zombie reads of the year... This is the single best zombie read I have laid my eyes on this year and sure to show up in my picks for best original graphic novel of the year... if you're a zombie fiend like myself, you should make it your single minded goal to seek out this book and digest then savor it."
MARK L. MILLAR, AIN'T IT COOL NEWS